STRETCHY
LIBRARY LESSONS

Reading Activities

Pat Miller

UpstartBooks

Fort Atkinson, Wisconsin

For Chris Miller,
generous in spirit and tenacious in effort.

Credits:
Pages 13–15: "The Three Armadillies Tuff" is adapted with permission from *The Three Armadillies Tuff* by Jackie Mims Hopkins. Illustrated by S. G. Brooks. Peachtree Publishers, Ltd., 2002.

Pages 30–31: "The Little Red Hen" story and illustrations are reprinted with permission from *Beyond Words: Great Stories for Hand and Voice* by Valerie Marsh. Highsmith Press, 1995.

Published by UpstartBooks
W5527 Highway 106
P.O. Box 800
Fort Atkinson, Wisconsin 53538-0800
1-800-448-4887

Contents

Introduction

In my 16 years as a school librarian, I have worked in three elementary libraries. None of them have had the same schedule, and they are probably all different from the one you have. In talking with library media specialists from across the country, I've discovered that the fixed schedule is very much a staple, despite the research and standards that urge "point of need" flexible library usage and scheduling.

Some school librarians have 45-minute classes, some only 30 minutes and some have a full hour. Class length even varies at the same school based on grade level, school events and school population. It also depends on whether or not librarians are part of "the rotation." If they are, the library serves as a class that students attend so teachers can have planning time.

The Stretchy Library Lessons series is designed to give you ideas for adapting lessons to fit your time constraints. Though the lessons are based on standards, they do not constitute a curriculum. Though they cross the elementary grade levels, they do not comprise enough lessons to get you through a semester. Instead, Stretchy Library Lessons gives you a wide variety of ways to pack a lot of learning into each lesson and to extend a short lesson with related games, Web sites, activities and other reading material.

How to Use This Book

Stretchy Library Lessons: Reading Activities has 10 basic lessons and 10 stretchy lessons. All of the lessons are designed to appeal to multiple intelligences, learning styles and reading abilities. The skills index on page 7 correlates each lesson by grade level and skill.

Each Stretchy Library Lesson includes:

- **Reading Skills.** These skills are in addition to the Key Reading Skills on page 6 and the Grade Appropriate Skills Index on page 7. They are taken from overlapping documents at the state and national level for English Language Arts.

- **A Range of Grades**. The lessons are K–5, though they can be adapted for preschoolers, special needs students and sixth graders.

- **A Purpose**. This helps library media specialists integrate the lessons with class curriculum, district and state media literacy standards and social and emotional goals.

- **The Format.** Listing the format (game, contest, read-aloud, etc.) helps you appeal to different learning styles.

- **A List of Materials.** These are readily available or easily made and should be gathered before you teach the lesson.

- **Items to Prepare in Advance.** If you teach all grades each day as I do, your lesson materials need to be well organized because there is little time between classes. This section tells you what needs to be made, purchased or found before a class comes in.

- **Twenty-Minute Activity.** My schedule is fixed at 30-minute intervals, with a few bands of flexible time that can be scheduled by any teacher. Allowing 10 minutes for students to select books, I try to design my basic class lesson to fit a 20-minute session. Most of the main activities can be taught in 20 minutes. The activities include all forms, worksheets and patterns that you will need.

- **The Stretchy Activity.** This activity extends the lesson to fit a longer time frame. If you have short classes like I do, the lessons in this book may be enough for 20 sessions. The stretchy activities include their own materials list, items to prepare in advance and steps for teaching the lesson.

- **Resources.** These books can be used instead of the featured title or as an extension. I tried to include newer works, all of which are in print and available from bookstores or online at press time. Always put these or similar books on display near your teaching area in case a teacher or child wants to extend their learning. The Web sites are current as of this printing, but if you get an error message, perform a keyword search on the Web site title. Be sure the title is enclosed in quotation marks.

Key Reading Skills

1. Draw conclusions, make inferences and predictions and determine cause and effect.

2. Represent text using story maps or graphic organizers.

3. Retell a story in sequence.

4. Present dramatic interpretation of the story.

5. Compare experience, feelings or point of view of characters across cultures.

6. React and respond to stories to reflect understanding.

7. Acquire information from books.

8. Use setting, characters and story structure to comprehend a story.

9. Listen and respond to a variety of literature through listening, reading, writing and creative activities.

10. Recognize fact and opinion; main idea and supporting details; and compare and contrast.

Grade Appropriate Skills Index

Twenty-minute activities are in bold.

LESSON TITLE	GRADES							SKILLS									
	K	1	2	3	4	5		1	2	3	4	5	6	7	8	9	10
Using Voice in Reading and Writing			X	X	X	X				X	X		X			X	
Voice Practice			X	X	X	X		X			X		X				
Singing Teeth	X	X	X					X			X		X			X	
Dental Cause and Effect	X	X	X					X								X	
Helping Hands	X	X	X	X	X	X				X			X		X	X	
Story Sequence	X	X	X	X	X	X		X		X						X	
Comprehension Basketball			X	X	X	X		X					X	X		X	X
Basketball Overtime			X	X	X	X		X		X			X	X		X	X
Legend of the Bluebonnet				X	X	X		X		X		X			X	X	
Empathize with a Character's Feelings				X	X	X		X			X	X	X		X	X	
Lost Any Good Teeth Lately?	X	X	X					X		X			X	X		X	
Animals Have Teeth, Too	X	X	X										X			X	X
Using Graphic Organizers			X	X	X	X		X	X							X	X
Practice Makes Perfect			X	X	X	X		X	X							X	X
The Boy Who Cried Wolf	X	X	X					X		X		X			X	X	
Fracture Your Own Tale	X	X	X	X	X	X		X		X		X			X	X	
Comprehension Climb	X	X	X	X				X					X		X	X	
Onward and Upward	X	X	X	X				X					X		X	X	
Nonfiction Grabber	X	X	X	X	X	X		X						X			X
Mind Your Q's and A's				X	X	X		X						X			X

Using Voice in Reading and Writing

Reading Skills: Use characters and voice to understand story structure; retell a story in sequence; and present a dramatic interpretation of a story.

Grades: 2–5

Purpose: To identify voice as an author's tool in reading and writing and to use voice in retelling a story through reader's theater.

Format: Group Discussion, Reader's Theater

Materials:

- *The Three Armadillies Tuff* by Jackie Mims Hopkins (Peachtree Publishers, 2002)

- script from pages 13–15

- bookmarks from page 19

- headbands from pages 16–18 *(optional)*

Prepare in Advance: Make enough copies of the script for all of your readers, plus one for you and one for the teacher. On each copy, highlight the speaker's name and all of his or her lines. On the bookmark, add the call numbers of the books you own in your library. Photocopy and cut out a bookmark for each student. Make the headbands following the directions on page 16. Write the sentences below on separate strips, the board, a transparency or chart paper.

- a. *You look bad. You need help.*
- b. *Mercy! You poor thing! You need a buff-and-puff makeover.*

- a. *My sister is large.*
- b. *She's my big—and I do mean BIG—sister.*

- a. *Lilly is a great girl and a good dancer.*
- b. *Lilly is a humdinger of a gal who really knows how to shake her shell on the dance floor.*

Activity Directions:

1. Voice is a critical part of good writing and it makes literature come alive. Use this lesson to help students understand what is meant by this elusive quality.

2. Compare the sentence pairs. Each pair says the same thing in a different voice. Which one gives you a mental picture of the speaker? Which sentence seems more alive? What makes the difference in these three examples? What would you guess about the first speaker (part of the country, gender, sense of humor, would you want for a friend)? The second? Why is voice so important in a story?

3. Tell the students that voice is critical in reader's theater. In this production, voice is the only thing that the actors have to bring the character to life. There are no costumes, no scenery and no special effects. It's the reader's voice that tells us about the character and about his or her emotions and personality.

4. Ask the teacher to appoint eight or nine readers, have the students volunteer for selected parts or distribute the scripts randomly. (If two readers are chosen for Tallula Coyote, the audience should be informed that there will be a change of readers.)

5. Tell the students to use what they've learned about voice as they silently read over their parts. Help them with unfamiliar words. Be sure the students know that the spelling connotes an accent so they should drop final letters where indicated and emphasize the words printed in capital letters. While readers review their lines, you may want to let the other students check out books.

6. Once the students are familiar with their parts, have them line up in story order, with the narrators on one side and the armadillos on the other. Tallula Coyote stands in the middle in her culvert tunnel. You should sit where you can prompt the readers if necessary. Hand out the headbands if you are using them.

7. Ask the audience to listen for words that add voice to the characters. Perform "The Three Armadillies Tuff."

8. Ask the audience what they remember about the voice of the characters. Ask the performers to add more information if needed.

9. Distribute the bookmarks. Students may want to indicate which adaptations they have read or hunt for the ones they haven't.

Voice Practice

Materials: None

Prepare in Advance: Write the italicized sentences where the class can see them.

- *I have always liked large pancakes with plenty of gooey syrup.*

- *I have ALWAYS liked large pancakes with plenty of gooey syrup.*

- *I have always liked LARGE pancakes with plenty of gooey syrup.*

- *I have always liked large PANCAKES with plenty of gooey syrup.*

- *I have always liked large pancakes with PLENTY of gooey syrup.*

- *I have always liked large pancakes with plenty of GOOEY syrup.*

Activity Directions:

1. Ask a student volunteer to say the following sentence in a variety of ways, using his or her voice to change the content.

   I have always liked large pancakes with plenty of gooey syrup.

   a. Say it as if you are nervous that you'll be punished for liking them.

   b. Say it as if you are disgusted with the whole messy stack.

   c. Say it as if you are bragging about what you like.

   d. How would it sound if you were mad that you weren't served your favorite breakfast?

2. Discuss how the message changes if you accent a different word. Have other volunteers read the sentences that you wrote out. They should emphasize the words in capital letters.

Resources

Books:

Bubba, the Cowboy Prince: A Fractured Texas Tale by Helen Ketteman. Scholastic, 1997. Loosely based on Cinderella, this story is set in Texas with a cow as the fairy godmother and Bubba, the stepson of a wicked rancher, as the hero.

The Horned Toad Prince by Jackie Mims Hopkins. Peachtree Publishers, 2000. In this retelling of *The Frog Prince,* a spunky cowgirl loses her new cowgirl hat and is helped by a horned toad on the understanding that she will do three small favors for him.

Web site:

Aaron Shepard's Reader's Theater
www.aaronshep.com/rt/index.html
Includes more than 24 ready-to-print scripts for folktales as well as instructions for teaching students to write their own reader's theater script.

Reader's Theater Script
The Three Armadillies Tuff

Adapted from *The Three Armadillies Tuff* by Jackie Mims Hopkins.
Illustrated by S. G. Brooks, Peachtree Ltd., 2002.

Readers: Narrator 1; Narrator 2; Narrator 3; Narrator 4; Lilly Armadilly Tuff (loves to dance); Jilly Armadilly Tuff (fashion queen); Dilly Armadilly Tuff (loves to eat); Tallula Coyote

Note: For an additional part, switch readers at the asterisk (*).

Narrator 1: Once there were three armadillo sisters named Tuff.

Narrator 2: The smallest was Lilly, a humdinger of a gal who really knew how to shake her shell on the dance floor.

Narrator 3: The middle sister was Jilly, the fashion queen of the family.

Narrator 4: The biggest sister was Dilly, who was crazy about chowin' down.

Narrator 1: The three sisters loved to have a good time!

Narrator 2: That's what led them to trouble one warm summer evening.

Lilly: Let's go to that new dance hall on the other side of the highway. I feel like kicking up my claws in some new dance steps.

Jilly: But if we run across the highway, I might chip my freshly painted toe-nails!

Dilly: Or get squashed by an 18-wheeler!

Lilly: Don't be such ninnies! We'll cut through the big drainpipe that runs under the road.

Narrator 3: The sisters agreed that this was a fine idea, so they waddled off to the highway.

Narrator 4: By and by, the sisters arrived at the culvert and peeked into the long, dark pipe.

Lilly: I'm not afraid. I'll go first.

Narrator 1: Scritch, scratch, scritch, scratch went Lilly's toenails on the metal drainpipe.

Stretchy Library Lessons: Reading Activities **13**

Tallula:	*(Use a growly voice)* Who's that scritch, scratchin' through my tunnel?
Lilly:	It's just me, Lilly Armadilly Tuff.
Tallula:	Come closer!
Narrator 2:	As Lilly stepped forward, she saw a skinny-legged coyote with hungry glaring eyes.
Lilly:	Whoo-wee! From the looks of your scrawny legs, I'd say you need a workout.
Tallula:	What I need is a nice hot bowl of armadilly chili.
Lilly:	Wait! My bigger sister is right behind me. She'd make a much better chili than I would.
Tallula:	Go on, then. Git!
Narrator 3:	Lilly scurried away before the coyote could change her mind.
Narrator 4:	Soon the second sister, Jilly, waddled into the tunnel. She was careful not to get cobwebs caught in her jewelry.
Jilly:	Scritch, scratch, scritch, scratch.
Tallula:	Who's that scritch, scratchin' through my tunnel?
Jilly:	It's just me, Jilly Armadilly Tuff.
Tallula:	Come closer!
Narrator 1:	Jilly stepped forward and noticed the drool dripping off the coyote's long tongue.
Jilly:	Yikes! That slobbery mouth of yours sure needs some lipstick! And your ratty old fur could use a bubble bath.
* **Tallula:**	What I NEED is a nice hot bowl of armadilly chili and some fancy armadilly skin boots.
Jilly:	Whoa! Hold on, fleabag. You'll be wantin' my big—and I do mean BIG—sister Dilly. Dilly will fill you up and make you a fine pair of boots. She might even fetch you a handbag!
Tallula:	A handbag? Hmmmmmm. Go on, then! Git!
Narrator 2:	Jilly skittered out of that tunnel lickety-split.
Narrator 3:	A few minutes later, the third sister SQUEEZED into the tunnel.

Dilly:	Scritch, scratch, scritch, scratch.
Tallula:	Who's that scritch, scratchin' through my tunnel?
Dilly:	It's just me, Dilly Armadilly Tuff. I'm trying to catch up with my sisters.
Tallula:	Well, your sisters aren't here. But they promised you'd make me a fine meal, some boots and a handbag.
Dilly:	Who, me? That's downright ridiculous. I can't cook or sew. But I DO know where we can find food and have some fun.
Narrator 4:	With a growl, the coyote stepped out of the shadows and Dilly got a good look at her.
Dilly:	Mercy! I mean, you POOR thing. How long has it been since you've had a girls' night out?
Tallula:	A what?
Dilly:	You know, a night out on the town with your friends.
Tallula:	*(Sadly)* I've always been alone. I don't have any friends.
Dilly:	Well, bless your little ol' heart. We can fix that! Come on, let's go find my sisters.
Narrator 1:	When Lilly and Jilly heard the coyote's sad story, the three sisters treated the pitiful critter to a fluff-and-puff makeover.
Narrator 2:	The coyote's name, by the way, was Tallula.
Narrator 3:	They treated Tallula to a fine meal at the garbage cans behind the Chomp and Stomp.
Narrator 4:	Before long, Tallula was looking fine in her new hair bow and lipstick, FAKE armadillo boots and a matching handbag.
Lilly:	Come on, girls, let me teach you the Armadilly Shuffle!
Narrator 1:	So if you hear critters digging through garbage cans …
Narrator 2:	or a coyote howling late at night …
Narrator 3:	don't you fret yourself none.
Narrator 4:	It's just Tallula and the Armadilly Tuff sisters having a rip-roarin' good time!

The End

Stretchy Library Lessons: Reading Activities

Headband Directions

1. Cut an 18" strip of construction paper for each headband.

2. Glue a character's picture or narrator nameplate to the center of each headband. Laminate the headbands for durability.

3. Since the headbands will be used multiple times, you want them to fit the largest head. Select a child with a large head. Wrap the headband to fit and staple. Children with smaller heads can tip the headband to fit.

Sample Narrator's Headband: Make one each for narrators 1–4.

Sample Character Headband: Make one for each character on pages 17 and 18.

Headband Patterns

Headband Patterns (continued)

Dilly

Tallula

Bookmark Patterns

Favorite Adaptations

Cinder Edna
(Ellen Jackson)

Cinderella Bigfoot
(Mike Thaler)

Cinderella Penguin
(Janet Perlman)

Cinderella's Rat
(Susan Meddaugh)

*Cindy Ellen:
A Wild Western Cinderella*
(Susan Lowell)

*The Cowboy and the
Black-Eyed Pea*
(Tony Johnston)

Joe Cinders
(Marianne Mitchell)

Peeping Beauty
(Mary Jane Auch)

Rufferella
(Vanessa Gill-Brown)

The Princess and the Pizza
(Mary Jane Auch)

The Three Little Javelinas
(Susan Lowell)

*The Three Little Wolves and
the Big Bad Pig*
(Eugene Trivizas)

The True Story of the 3 Little Pigs
(Jon Scieszka)

Favorite Adaptations

Cinder Edna
(Ellen Jackson)

Cinderella Bigfoot
(Mike Thaler)

Cinderella Penguin
(Janet Perlman)

Cinderella's Rat
(Susan Meddaugh)

*Cindy Ellen:
A Wild Western Cinderella*
(Susan Lowell)

*The Cowboy and the
Black-Eyed Pea*
(Tony Johnston)

Joe Cinders
(Marianne Mitchell)

Peeping Beauty
(Mary Jane Auch)

Rufferella
(Vanessa Gill-Brown)

The Princess and the Pizza
(Mary Jane Auch)

The Three Little Javelinas
(Susan Lowell)

*Three Little Wolves and the
Big Bad Pig*
(Eugene Trivizas)

The True Story of the 3 Little Pigs
(Jon Scieszka)

Favorite Adaptations

Cinder Edna
(Ellen Jackson)

Cinderella Bigfoot
(Mike Thaler)

Cinderella Penguin
(Janet Perlman)

Cinderella's Rat
(Susan Meddaugh)

*Cindy Ellen:
A Wild Western Cinderella*
(Susan Lowell)

*The Cowboy and the
Black-Eyed Pea*
(Tony Johnston)

Joe Cinders
(Marianne Mitchell)

Peeping Beauty
(Mary Jane Auch)

Rufferella
(Vanessa Gill-Brown)

The Princess and the Pizza
(Mary Jane Auch)

The Three Little Javelinas
(Susan Lowell)

*Three Little Wolves and the
Big Bad Pig*
(Eugene Trivizas)

The True Story of the 3 Little Pigs
(Jon Scieszka)

Singing Teeth

Reading Skills: To listen to texts read aloud, react and respond to stories to reflect understanding, make predictions and determine cause and effect.

Grades: K–2

Purpose: To practice using ordinal numbers, share stories of losing teeth, enjoy a humorous story and make an origami tooth pocket for the tooth fairy. You may want to do this activity for National Children's Dental Health Month in February.

Format: Flannel Board Rhyme, Song, Read-Aloud

Materials:

- flannel or magnetic board (see sidebar)

- flannel mouth and teeth patterns (see page 24)

- felt

- hook and loop tape or magnetic tape

- *Andrew's Loose Tooth* by Robert Munsch (Scholastic, 1999)

- copy of "Ten Little Baby Teeth" song (see page 26)

Prepare in Advance: Photocopy the mouth and teeth patterns, then cut the shapes out of felt. If you use a flannel board, attach the hook side of the hook and loop tape to the back of the mouth. Do the same with the back of the teeth using very small pieces of tape. Attach the soft side of the hook and loop tape to the front of the flannel mouth. If you are using a magnetic board, attach larger pieces of magnetic tape to the outside edges of the mouth and small pieces to each tooth. Locate the book. Make photocopies of the song.

Activity Directions:

1. Ask the students about the best ways to take care of their teeth (go to the dentist, eat good foods, drink milk, brush and floss daily, avoid sugary snacks, etc.).

2. Ask the students if they have lost any of their baby teeth. Have them hold up a finger for each

---

Recipe for a Magnetic Flannel Board
Idea from Caroline Feller Bauer

You'll need:

- large metal drip pan (found in the automotive section of a discount department store)
- newspaper
- pencil
- scissors
- 1 yard black felt
- black spray paint
- Tacky glue
- 1-inch foam paintbrush
- 4½ yards of glittery trim
- 12 clothespins

1. Trace the back edge of the drip pan onto newspaper to make a pattern. Use the pattern to cut out a piece of felt.

2. Spray the back of the pan with black paint.

3. Use the foam brush to generously apply glue to the front of the drip pan.

4. Attach the black felt. Smooth it out, then allow it to dry.

5. Run a thick line of glue around the inside edge of the drip pan. Attach the trim, pressing it firmly into place. Allow a little extra trim in the curves of the pan.

6. Use clothespins to hold the trim in place while it dries.

tooth they have lost. Ask two or three students to tell how they were able to get their loose teeth out.

3. For grade 2, hand out photocopies of the song. Use the flannel mouth to chant the "Ten Little Baby Teeth" song. As you remove each tooth, place it on the board in a row to review ordinal numbers. Every third tooth or so, review the lost teeth by pointing to them and saying, "Here's the first, the second, etc." At the end, count from 1 to 10 and then reverse, using ordinal numbers.

4. Read *Andrew's Loose Tooth*. Do the telling of this exaggerated slapstick story in a larger-than-life manner. Encourage the children to join you in pantomiming the refrain where Andrew reaches out, grabs an apple, polishes it on his shirt and bites into it. Make a chomping face. Then everyone says loudly, "EEE YOWWW!" Also have them do the refrain, "Ooh, ooh, ooh. You DO have a loose tooth and I know just what to do." Students will enjoy when the dentist's car falls apart and the tooth fairy takes a hammer to Andrew's tooth.

5. Before turning each page, encourage students to predict what the character will do next.

Dental Cause and Effect

Materials:

- Cause and Effect Chart on poster board or a transparency (see example on page 25)

- pen

- chalk or water-based overhead pen

Prepare in Advance: Make a blank chart similar to the example on page 25, with causes in one column and effects in the other. Have each cause and effect from the example listed on a strip of paper or transparency. Attach double-sided tape so they can be placed on the chart. Display the chart in a place where it can be seen by the entire class.

Activity Directions:

1. Review the sequence of the story by having students sort the causes in the correct order, then attach them to the chart.

2. Check to be sure the sequence is correct, then have the students match the causes and effects.

Just for Fun: Origami Tooth Fairy Pocket

Materials:

- 8½" square of paper for each student

- stickers or tape

- white party mints or other small edible treat

Prepare in Advance: Cut enough paper squares to have one for each student. Find stickers or adhesive tape to seal each pocket.

Activity Directions:

Follow the diagram on page 23 to make a pocket for a lost tooth. Students can slip it under their pillow for the tooth fairy.

1. Have the students fold the paper in half, corner to corner, so they have a triangle shape. Crease the fold.

2. Fold the left point to touch just below the midpoint of the right side.

3. Fold the right point to touch just below the midpoint of the left side.

4. Fold down a single flap so it covers the folded "arms." Tape down if desired.

5. Poke fingers gently into the opening. One flap should remain up.

6. Give each child a white party mint (to substitute as a tooth) to put in the pocket.

7. Fold over the remaining flap to close the pocket.

8. Adhere a sticker or piece of tape to seal the pocket shut.

Resources

Books:

Grandpa's Teeth by Rod Clement. HarperCollins Children's Books, 1999. The search is on for grandpa's lost dentures. They can't be found until the dog gives an amazingly human smile at the end of the book.

Little Rabbit's Loose Tooth by Lucy Bate. Crown Books for Young Readers, 1983. Little Rabbit waits impatiently to lose her tooth and imagines all the things that can be done with the tooth when it comes out.

Throw Your Tooth on the Roof: Tooth Traditions from Around the World by Selby B. Beeler. Houghton Mifflin, 2001. Though the tooth fairy is not a worldwide tradition, doing something with your tooth besides throwing it in the trash is universal.

Web site:

To Tell the Tooth
www.ada.org/public/games/totell/totelltooth.swf
Play an interactive game with Al Smiles from the American Dental Association.

Origami Tooth Fairy Pocket

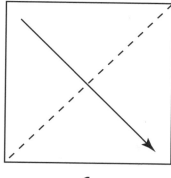

1

Fold paper in half, corner to corner. You should have a triangle shape. Crease the fold with your fingers.

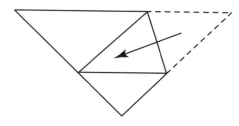

2

Fold the left point to touch just below the midpoint of the right side.

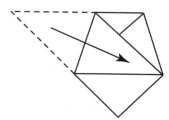

3

Fold the right point to touch just below the midpoint of the left side.

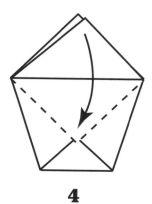

4

Fold down a single flap so it covers the folded "arms." Tape down if desired.

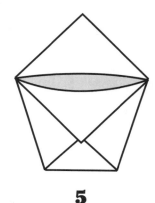

5

Poke fingers gently into the opening. One flap should remain up.

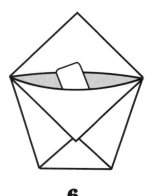

6

Put your tooth (or a piece of candy) into the pocket.

7

Fold over the remaining flap to close the pocket.

8

Seal the pocket shut with a sticker if you wish.

Flannel Mouth and Teeth Patterns

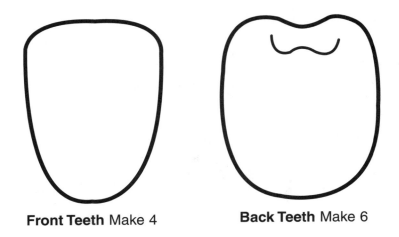

Front Teeth Make 4

Back Teeth Make 6

Tooth patterns are actual size.

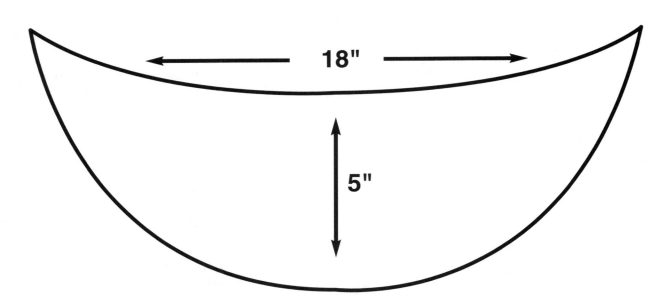

18"

5"

Smile Pattern: Enlarge to dimensions shown.

Sample Cause and Effect Chart

Andrew's Loose Tooth
by Robert Munsch

Cause	Effect
Andrew bit an apple.	His tooth hurt so much he couldn't eat.
Andrew's mom pulled his tooth with both hands.	She couldn't pull his loose tooth out.
Andrew's tooth would not come out when his dad pulled it with pliers.	Andrew's dad put his foot on Andrew's nose so he could pull harder.
The dentist tied Andrew's tooth to his car bumper.	The whole car fell apart.
Andrew's mom, dad and dentist could not pull out his stubborn tooth.	Andrew had to skip breakfast.
Andrew could not eat his breakfast.	He sat in his front yard looking sad.
Louis called the tooth fairy.	The tooth fairy came right away on her motorcycle.
The tooth fairy clanged Andrew's loose tooth.	The hammer broke into two pieces.
Louis shook pepper up Andrew's nose.	Andrew sneezed.
Andrew sneezed.	The tooth shot across town till the tooth fairy caught it.

Ten Little Baby Teeth
by Pat Miller

Ten little baby teeth smiling big and fine,
First one fell out and then there were nine.

Nine little baby teeth chewing so great,
Second one fell out and then there were eight.

Eight little baby teeth belong to Kevin,
Third one fell out and then there were seven.

Seven little baby teeth crunching carrot sticks,
Fourth one fell out and then there were six.

Six little baby teeth, sakes alive!
Fifth one fell out and then there were five.

Five little baby teeth chomping on some more,
Sixth one fell out and then there were four.

Four little baby teeth bit my knee,
Seventh one fell out and then there were three.

Three little baby teeth, here's a clue—
Eighth one fell out and then there were two.

Two little baby teeth chewed a bun,
Ninth one fell out and then there was one.

One little baby tooth, the loneliest one,
It fell out and then there were none.

But lucky for me, I'm not toothless Jack.
Before I knew it, new ones grew back!

Helping Hands

Reading Skills: To present dramatic interpretation of a story, recognize genre features of folktales and retell a story in sequence.

Grades: K–5

Purpose: To share a folktale and its characteristics, learn that not all people speak with their voices and enjoy a story using sign language.

Format: Storytelling with American Sign Language

Materials:

- "The Little Red Hen" story and illustrations from *Beyond Words: Great Stories for Hand and Voice* by Valerie Marsh (reprinted on pages 30–31)

- story sequence sheet (see page 32)

- puppets of a chicken, pig, cat and dog to use with your student leaders *(optional)*

Prepare in Advance: Photocopy "The Little Red Hen" illustrations to keep near you for reference. Learn the story so you can recite it comfortably. Keep the story sequence sheet near you in case you lose track while telling the story.

Activity Directions:

1. Explain that not all storytelling is done with the voice and that not all stories are enjoyed with the ears. Today we are going to tell a story together using our hands. We will listen to it with our eyes and ears.

2. Before telling the story, teach students the signs from "The Little Red Hen." Instead of telling the entire story in sign, the class will use 11 signs for some of the things in the story.

3. Tell the story, stopping to do the signs as needed. Most students know the story by heart so the interruptions will not hurt the flow of the story. If you are using puppets, have the student leaders sign with one hand and use the puppet with the other.

Story Sequence

Materials:

- set of story sequence cards for each student (see page 33)

- envelope for each student

- set of enlarged story sequence cards for display

- flannel or magnetic board

- hook and loop tape or magnets

Prepare in Advance: Make a set of story sequence cards for each child by photocopying the cards on page 33 onto colored paper. Cut them out and place each set in an envelope. Make an additional set in a larger size for the flannel or magnetic board. Color the pictures and attach hook and loop tape or a magnet to each card.

Activity Directions:

Have the students put their cards in the correct order. Check their answers by attaching a set of cards to the flannel or magnetic board or stand them on a chalkboard rail.

Resources

Books:

Cook-a-Doodle-Doo! by Susan Stevens Crummel. Harcourt, 1999. In this version, the grand chick of *The Little Red Hen* is making strawberry shortcake with her friends who DO try to help, but with disastrous and funny results. A recipe for strawberry shortcake is included.

Everybody Bakes Bread by Norah Dooley. Lerner Publishing Group, 1996. Includes seven recipes for international varieties of breads in this story of a multinational community.

Little Red Hen (Makes a Pizza) by Philemon Sturges. Penguin Putnam Books for Young Readers, 2002. This time the Little Red Hen craves a pizza and still has to deal with unhelpful neighbors.

Sun Bread by Elisa Kleven. Penguin Putnam Books for Young Readers, 2001. Rhyming text explains how the owner of Fiesta Bakery spreads winter cheer with a sun-shaped loaf of bread and lots of love.

Web sites:

American Sign Language
where.com/scott.net/asl/
This site lets you teach yourself sign language with an animated fingerspelling dictionary, a converter that changes the word you type into fingerspelling and an interactive quiz.

Learn to Sign with Koko
www.koko.org/world/signlanguage.html
Watch a video of Koko the gorilla using American Sign Language.

Botham Bakery's Guide to Bread: From Seed to Sandwich
www.botham.co.uk/seed/first.htm
A fun and interesting site where students can find out how bread is made, learn about its history, play games or try out a variety of bread recipes. Includes a section for teachers.

The Little Red Hen

Reprinted from *Beyond Words: Great Stories for Hand and Voice* by Valerie Marsh.

*L*ong ago, there was a **Little Red Hen**. She was friends with a **duck**, a **cat** and a **dog**. The **Little Red Hen** worked hard all day long. But the **duck**, the **cat** and the **dog did not**! They **did not** like to **help**.

One fine spring day, **Little Red Hen** found some grains of **wheat**. She took them home. She asked, "Who will **help** me plant these grains of **wheat**?"

"**Not I**," said **Duck**.

"**Not I**," said **Cat**.

"**Not I**," said **Dog**.

"Very well then, I'll plant the seeds myself," said **Little Red Hen**. And she **did**.

One fine summer day, **Little Red Hen** went out to the garden. She saw that the **wheat** was growing. She asked, "Who will **help** me water the **wheat** and pull the weeds?"

"**Not I**," said **Duck**.

"**Not I**," said **Cat**.

"**Not I**," said **Dog**.

"Very well then, I'll water the **wheat** and pull the weeds myself," said **Little Red Hen**. And she **did**.

One fine fall day, **Little Red Hen** went out to the garden. She saw that the **wheat** was very tall and golden. She asked, "Who will **help** me cut down the **wheat**?"

"**Not I**," said **Duck**.

"**Not I**," said **Cat**.

"**Not I**," said **Dog**.

"Very well then, I'll cut the **wheat** myself," said **Little Red Hen**. And she **did**. **Little Red Hen** scooped the **wheat** into her wagon and asked, "Who will **help** me take this **wheat** to the mill? It must be ground into flour."

"**Not I**," said **Duck**.

"**Not I**," said **Cat**.

"**Not I**," said **Dog**.

"Very well then, I'll take it myself," said **Little Red Hen**. And she **did**.

One fine winter day, **Little Red Hen** walked into her kitchen. She saw the **wheat** flour. She said, "This day is a good day to bake. I will bake a loaf of bread with the **wheat** flour. Who will **help** me bake the bread?"

"**Not I**," said **Duck**.

"**Not I**," said **Cat**.

"**Not I**," said **Dog**.

"Very well then, I'll bake it myself," said **Little Red Hen**. And she **did**.

Soon **Duck** smelled the baking bread. Soon **Cat** smelled the baking bread. Soon **Dog** smelled the baking bread.

When the bread was all done, **Little Red Hen** said, "Who will **help** me eat the bread?"

"I will!" said **Duck**.

"I will!" said **Cat**.

"I will!" said **Dog**.

"But who planted the **wheat**? Who watered the **wheat** and pulled the weeds? Who cut the **wheat**? Who took the **wheat** to the mill to be ground into flour? Who baked the bread?" asked **Little Red Hen**.

"**Not I**," said **Duck**.

"**Not I**," said **Cat**.

"**Not I**," said **Dog**.

"Very well then, I'll eat the bread myself." And she **did**.

Little

"L"-shape hands, index tips out, then move close together.

Red

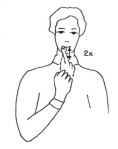

Brush lower lip twice with RH "R" sign.

Hen

"Three"-shape RH. Tap thumb on chin.

Duck

Snap thumb, index and middle fingers together at mouth.

Cat

Place thumb and index of RH "9" at side of upper lip. Pull away twice.

Dog

Pat right thigh twice, then snap fingers twice.

Not

RH knuckle left, "A"-shape. Place extended thumb under chin, then move out.

Did

Move open hands, palms down, from side to side. Then swing RH open "B," tips forward, twice.

Help

Place LH "A," thumb up, in RH palm. Raise both hands.

Wheat

LH, palm up, "5" shape, fingers cupped. Brush fourth finger of RH "W" up against LH fingers. Repeat.

I

Palm left, "I"-shape RH, then place thumb side on chest.

The Little Red Hen Storytelling Sequence

Introduce the hen, duck, cat and dog.

1. Hen works hard, the rest don't.

2. In the spring, Hen finds wheat and asks for help to plant.

3. All say, "Not I." She plants it herself.

4. In the summer she asks for help to water and pull weeds.

5. All say, "Not I." She waters and weeds it herself.

6. In the fall, Hen needs help to cut the wheat.

7. All say, "Not I." She cuts it herself.

8. Then she needs help to take it to the mill to be made into flour.

9. All say, "Not I." She takes it herself.

10. In the winter, Hen needs help to make the wheat flour into bread and asks for help.

11. All say, "Not I." She bakes it herself.

12. All smell the baking bread. Hen asks for help to eat it.

13. All say, "I will!" Then she asks who did all the work.

14. They all have to say, "Not I." So Hen eats the bread herself.

Story Sequence Cards

Spring—Hen finds wheat, "Who will help me plant?"	**"Not I," they said.**	**Summer—"Who will help me water and weed?"**
"Not I," they said.	**Fall—"Who will help me cut the wheat?"**	**"Not I," they said.**
Winter—"Who will help me bake the bread?"	**"Not I," they said.**	**"Then I will bake it and eat it myself," she said. And she did!**

Comprehension Basketball

Reading Skills: To learn fact and opinion; main idea and supporting details; and compare and contrast.

Grades: 2–5

Purpose: To practice reading comprehension in a fun format as well as the test format used in standardized reading.

Format: Game

Materials:

- *Bubba, the Cowboy Prince: A Fractured Texas Tale* by Helen Ketteman (Scholastic, 1997) for grades 2–3

- *Joey Pigza Swallowed the Key* by Jack Gantos (HarperCollins Children's Books, 2000) for grades 4–5

- questions from page 37 or page 38 (depending on grade level)

- overhead transparencies of noted pages from the book

- basketball with hoop (available at dollar stores) or small foam basketball and a trash can

- 2 sets of 5 paper squares (each set should be a different color)

- masking tape or thick yarn

- pencil for each student

- paper strip for each student to use as answer sheet

Prepare in Advance: Make a transparency of several pages from the appropriate book (pages are noted on question sheets). Number the paragraphs, then make a photocopy for each student. Set up a basketball game by attaching the hoop to a chalkboard or whiteboard or setting the trash can on a table. Number the paper squares from 1 to 5. (If time allows for more questions, include more squares and numbers.) Set up the foul line after allowing several students to shoot trial baskets. Gauge the point where students have the most success getting a basket and mark it on the floor with tape or yarn.

Note: If you like, you may use a book of your choosing and write questions following the format of those on pages 37–38.

Activity Directions:

1. Before this lesson, the appropriate book should be read to the class. Divide the class into two teams.

2. Show the transparency of a page from the book. Have the students reread their copy. The object of the game is to name the paragraph that gives them the correct information to answer the question.

3. Ask the first team a question and read all three answer choices aloud. The students need to choose the correct answer, then look at their excerpt to find the paragraph that answers that question. The students can jot their answers down on the strip of paper.

4. The team must give the letter of the correct answer and the correct paragraph number. Then they read the sentence that gives the answer. If the answer is correct, the team gets the paper square that corresponds with the question number. If the answer is incorrect, the question rebounds to the second team. If the rebound is answered correctly, they get the other team's corresponding paper square. Then they get to answer their own question. If they miss the rebound, the corresponding paper square is placed aside and they answer their own question.

5. Alternate questions between teams. A student who has previously answered may not answer again unless no one on the team can respond.

6. After all of the questions are answered, students come to the line on the floor. Each team gets to shoot as many baskets as they can in a predetermined amount of time, using different team members for each shot. Baskets earn one point for the team.

7. The team with the most points (cards plus baskets) makes their book selections first, gets an additional book over the usual limit or receives a small bookmark or treat.

Basketball Overtime

Materials:

- sentences of sequential events from page 39 or 40

- magnetic strips

- magnetic board

Prepare in Advance: Reproduce the sentences or use events from a book of your choosing. Include two events that did not happen. Cut the sheet apart so the sentences are in strips. Attach a magnetic strip to each one. Scramble the sentences on the magnetic board.

Activity Directions:

1. Have the teams take turns putting the events in order from first to last. Tell the students that there are two incorrect events so they need to think carefully.

2. Each time a team takes a turn, they get to take a shot at the basket. The teams get one point for each event they put in the correct order and one point for each basket they make. The team with the most points at the end wins.

Time Saving Tip

I have taught as many as 10 sections of each grade—this involves a lot of repetition. So for my time, I like to make teaching devices that can be used with multiple classes over many years. I use a lot of sentence strips for the various grades. To make them easy to reuse for another lesson, I store them in pocket file folders labeled with the name of the story. They are then filed alphabetically by the title. If you use long strips that need to be folded to fit a folder, consider purchasing a sentence strip storage box. Available at teacher supply stores, the box is long and narrow and has divider tabs made especially for sentence strips.

Resources

Web sites:

Attention Deficit Hyperactivity Disorder
www.brainpop.com/health/nervous/adhd/index.weml
Like the students in *Joey Pigza Swallowed the Key,* your own students may be confused by ADHD. This site gives interesting and clear explanations of the disability and its manifestations. Such knowledge may make it easier for an ADHD student to be accepted by his or her peers and give your other students more compassion for those with ADHD.

TeachingBooks
www.teachingbooks.net
This site is a gold mine for connecting students with their favorite authors. It contains original five-minute videos of authors and illustrators (filmed in their studios or where they write), teacher's guides for thousands of children's books (searchable by author, illustrator or title) and links to Web sites for authors, illustrators, book awards and more. It includes instructions and downloads for the programs needed to view the videos—and it is free.

Bubba, the Cowboy Prince
by Helen Ketteman
Comprehension Questions for Grades 2–3

Note: For shorter passages like pages 5 and 8 in this book, you may only need a printed copy for special needs students. Others can read directly from the transparencies.

SKILL	QUESTION
Page 5—"Now, Miz Lurleen…"	
Details (b)	**Who was Miz Lurleen?** a. a school teacher b. rich ranch owner c. Bubba's aunt
Inference (a)	**Why did Miz Lurleen want to marry?** a. She didn't want to be lonely. b. She needed someone to inherit her money. c. She loved weddings.
Details (c)	**What was her most important qualification for a husband?** a. He had to be rich also. b. He had to be handsome. c. He had to love ranching.
Cause and Effect (b)	**Why were Texas ranchers invited to Miz Lurleen's house?** a. She wanted to buy their cattle. b. She was looking for a husband. c. She wanted to have a big barbecue.
Fact/Opinion (a)	**Which of these is an opinion?** a. Miz Lurleen was the most beautiful woman in the county. b. Miz Lurleen was the richest woman in the county. c. Miz Lurleen was the youngest rancher in the county.
Page 8— "By the time…"	
Fact/Opinion (c)	**Which is a fact?** a. Dwayne and Milton were mean. b. Cattle smell bad. c. Bubba wanted to go to the dance.
Details (b)	**How do we know Bubba smelled stinky?** a. His shirt was raggedy. b. Milton said he smelled worse than a cow. c. Bubba had been working on the ranch.
Main Idea/Details (a)	**Why did Bubba ride out into a storm?** a. He wanted to see how the cattle were doing. b. He wanted to wash his dirty cowboy clothes. c. He was taking a shortcut to Miz Lurleen's ranch.
Inference (c)	**Why was Bubba upset when he rode away from the house?** a. He was mad at his stepbrothers. b. His feelings were hurt because Dwayne made fun of him. c. He was sad that he wasn't good enough for Miz Lurleen.

Joey Pigza Swallowed the Key
by Jack Gantos
Comprehension Questions for Grades 4–5

SKILL	QUESTION
The last paragraph on page 69, all of page 70 and the remainder of the last paragraph that continues onto page 71.	
Inference (a)	**Joey's reaction to Mrs. Cole's speech to the gifted class** a. showed he wanted to help others b. embarrassed the nurse c. caused the class to laugh
Fact/Opinion (b)	**Which is an opinion?** a. Joey had trouble concentrating. b. Joey made funny jokes. c. The nurse liked Joey.
Main Idea/Details (b)	**While Joey was hiding behind stage, he got a good idea** a. when he read a sign posted on the nearby wall b. from the lady speaking on stage c. when he heard the kids in the audience laughing
Inference (c)	**How do we know Joey didn't like being in trouble?** a. He cried when the principal talked to him. b. He hid his bad notes from his mother. c. He liked getting along with others.
Details (b)	**How do we know the nurse liked Joey?** a. She gave him candy. b. She wrapped his ankle. c. She sent a good note to his mother.
Fact/Opinion (c)	**Which of these is a fact?** a. Joey's school nurse was the best. b. Joey enjoyed misbehaving. c. Joey's ankle was hurting.
Inference (a)	**How do we know Joey was not easily embarrassed?** a. He wore a rabbit slipper in the hall. b. He swallowed a key. c. He loved to make his classmates laugh.
Details (c)	**So he wouldn't reveal his hiding place on stage, Joey clapped by** a. wiggling his fingers b. hitting his hand on the curtain c. blinking his eyes
Inference (a)	**Which is true?** a. Joey liked to make the nurse laugh. b. Joey did not like wearing shoes. c. The nurse was mad that Joey came to the clinic so often.

Sequence of Events

Bubba, the Cowboy Prince: A Fractured Texas Tale by Helen Ketteman

Bubba lived on a ranch he loved with Dwayne and Milton and his wicked stepdaddy.

The stepbrothers bossed Bubba around every day.

Miz Lurleen decided to throw a ball to find someone to marry and to help run her ranch.

Milton and Dwayne spent the day getting gussied up for the ball.

Poor exhausted Bubba was left behind when his stepbrothers drove off to the ball.

Bubba sadly went off into the storm to check on the cattle.

Bubba's fairy godcow swished her tail and changed his raggedy clothes into handsome ones.

Bubba rode to the ball on a steer that had been changed into a white stallion.

Bubba danced with Miz Lurleen and won her heart.

At midnight, Bubba was embarrassed to find himself dirty and stinky again.

Miz Lurleen searched from ranch to ranch trying to find the owner of a dirty cowboy boot.

Milton and Dwayne had chicken fits when the boot fit Bubba.

Miz Lurleen and Bubba rode off into the sunset and lived happily ever after.

* The fairy godcow changed some mice into horses.

* Bubba's wicked stepdaddy made Bubba wash the outside of the house.

* = *non-event*

Sequence of Events

Joey Pigza Swallowed the Key by Jack Gantos

Mrs. Maxy sent Joey out of the room for repeatedly saying, "Can I get back to you on that?"

Grandma wanted Joey to get in the refrigerator so he could cool down.

Joey hurt himself by putting his finger in the pencil sharpener and turning the handle.

Joey swallowed his house key after Mrs. Maxy cut off its string.

Joey was put in Mrs. Howard's special ed class in the basement.

Joey helped Harold by blowing out his birthday candles.

Joey jumped off a barn roof rafter during the class trip to Amish country.

When he sneaked into a special program, Joey decided to do something to make the world a better place.

Joey cut off the tip of Maria Dombrowski's nose.

Mrs. Jarzab, the principal, suspended Joey for six weeks and sent him to a Special Ed Center.

Joey's mother promised him a dog if he did well in his new special ed class.

Joey met a boy named Charlie who only had tiny stumps for arms.

* Joey visited his dad for the weekend and tried to explain why he cut off Maria's nose.

* Mrs. Maxy told the principal that she never wanted Joey back in her class.

* = *non-event*

© 2003 by Pat Miller (UpstartBooks)

Legend of the Bluebonnet

Reading Skills: To listen critically to interpret and evaluate, make inferences and predictions, represent text using a timeline, analyze character traits and feelings and compare experience of characters across cultures.

Grades: 3–5 (Can be used with younger grades as well.)

Purpose: To share how courage and selflessness are esteemed across cultures and to understand the value of sacrifice for another.

Format: Read Aloud, Discussion, Re-enactment and Craft

Materials:

- *The Legend of the Bluebonnet: An Old Tale of Texas* by Tomie dePaola (Putnam, 1996)

- pictures of the Comanche Indians, their dwellings and clothing

- United States map

- silk bluebonnets or pictures of them

- sentence strips

- magnetic strips

- magnetic board

Prepare in Advance: Use the Web site listed on page 44 or a book to locate the territory of the Comanche Indians. Use pins to mark the territory on the map. Set up a display of related titles, including other Indian legends (see page 44) and books on Comanche and other Plains Indians. Photocopy the events on page 45, then cut them into sentence strips. Attach a magnetic strip to each one. Scramble the sentences on the magnetic board.

Activity Directions:

1. Share pictures and/or artifacts of Comanche life. Locate their home on the map and discuss what life was like for them. Explain that a legend is a story that may have begun in fact and is used to explain how or why something happened.

2. Read *The Legend of the Bluebonnet* aloud to the class.

3. Show the students the bluebonnets, then have them think about an object of their own that is very precious. Is it something they would take if they could only save one thing from their belongings? Why is it so important? How would they feel if they were asked to give it up for someone else?

4. Have the students arrange the sentence strips in order on the magnetic board. Then have them note which events were causes and which were effects.

Empathize with a Character's Feelings

Materials:

- markers

- scissors

- bottles of white glue

- trash can

- red and yellow paper

- one set of the following for each student:

    - paper lunch sack

    - 3 18" strips of black crepe paper

    - 2 12" pieces of colorful yarn

    - several colored beads

    - blue feather or blue tissue paper

    - sheet of tissue paper or newspaper

Prepare in Advance: Gather all of the materials for the students and put them into the lunch sacks for easy distribution. Have the markers, scissors and glue in boxes or bins that can be shared. Decorate the trash can with red and yellow paper to resemble a fire.

Activity Directions:

1. Have each child make a Bluebonnet Doll following the directions below.

   a. Decorate four inches of the sack, starting from the opening, as the hem of the doll's dress.

   b. Draw the doll's facial features on the bottom third of the sack. Place the eyes at the fold line.

   c. Loosely crumple a sheet of tissue or newspaper. Put it inside the sack to fill the head.

   d. Thread the beads on one of the 12" strands of yarn.

   e. Tie off the head with this necklace. Make sure all of the stuffing is above the necklace and that the beads are below the "chin." Don't tie the yarn too tight or the head will flop over. Trim the surplus yarn.

   f. Cut the other piece of yarn in half.

   g. Bunch the strips of crepe paper together and tie them one inch from the end with the 6" piece of yarn.

   h. Braid the crepe paper. Tie the braid off with the other 6" strand.

   i. Tie the feather at the end of one of the braids. If you are using tissue paper, cut a piece into a feather shape, then tie it to one of the braids.

   j. Squeeze a thick line of glue across the top of the sack. Attach the braid and hold it until it stays.

2. Retell the part of the story where She-Who-Is-Alone burned her doll to bring the rain for her people. Tell the students that they are going to re-enact that sacrifice. Put the fire-decorated trash can in the front of the group. Tell the students that each person is going to throw their doll into the fire. At the end of the day, they will be burned in the school's trash incinerator.

3. Ask who would like to go first. Pause. My experience has been that no one will want to be first. After a moment, talk about how no one wanted to lose their doll—a doll that was made of simple materials and that they have only owned for a few minutes. Imagine how much more difficult the sacrifice would be if this doll was the only thing they had left of their parents, their only company and their only family.

4. Pause a little for thinking time, then tell them they may each keep their Bluebonnet Dolls as a reminder of the great importance of thinking of others.

Resources

Books:

Between Earth and Sky: Legends of Native American Sacred Places by Joseph Bruchac. Harcourt, 1999.

Dancing Drum: A Cherokee Legend by Terri Cohlene. Troll, 1991. Part of the Native American Legend series that includes *Clamshell Boy: A Makah Legend* and *Ka-Ha-Si and the Loon: An Eskimo Legend.*

How the Stars Fell Into the Sky: A Navajo Legend by Jerrie Oughton. Houghton Mifflin, 1996.

The Legend of the Indian Paintbrush by Tomie dePaola. Putnam, 1991.

The Messenger of Spring: A Chippewa, Ojibwa Legend by C. J. Taylor. Tundra Books, 1997.

Web sites:

Quanah Parker—A Texas Legend
www.lnstar.com/mall/texasinfo/quanah.htm
Short biography and photo of the last chief of the Comanches, who never lost a battle to the white man.

The Texas Comanches
www.texasindians.com/comanche.htm
Includes information and pictures, particularly a map showing the tribe's migration over 300 years.

Sequence of Events

The Legend of the Bluebonnet
by Tomie dePaola

Beginning

One young Indian girl loses both her parents to a terrible disease.	**cause**
The tribe renames the young girl She-Who-Is-Alone.	**effect**
A drought brings much suffering to the tribe.	**cause**
The wise men pray for wisdom about how to end the drought.	**effect**

Middle

The wise men receive a message that rain will come if the tribe makes a great sacrifice.	**cause**
She-Who-Is Alone sacrifices her doll.	**effect**
She-Who-Is Alone scatters the ashes left from her doll.	**cause**

End

The ashes become bluebonnet flowers.	**effect**
Her tribe discovers the great sacrifice that She-Who-Is-Alone made for them.	**cause**
The tribe renames her She-Who-Loves-Her-People.	**effect**

Stretchy Library Lessons: Reading Activities **45**

Lost Any Good Teeth Lately?

Reading Skills: To react and respond to stories to reflect understanding and acquire information from books.

Grades: K–2

Purpose: To learn about our teeth and how they work.

Format: Song, Creative Dramatics, Game

Materials:

- *How Many Teeth?* by Paul Showers (HarperCollins Children's Books, 1991)

- yellow and green paper

- "Brush, Brush, Brush Your Teeth" song (see page 48)

Prepare in Advance: Make a copy of the song and the questions on page 49. Cut square cards out of yellow and green paper, one pair per student.

Activity Directions:

1. Discuss the best ways for the students to brush their teeth (down from the gums on top, up from the gums on the bottom, side to side across the chewing surfaces). Tell them that we are going to sing a song and act out being toothbrushes.

2. Have the students stand an arm's length apart in a circle. Sing the song "Brush Your Teeth" (page 48) as they act out brushing. Have them squat for "brush them down" and jump up for "brush them up." Swing arms back and forth across the body for "brush them side to side." Repeat the song several times, encouraging the children to sing with you.

3. Give each child a yellow and a green card. These are their yes/no cards. Yellow is YES and green is NO.

4. Ask the children if they know how to take care of their teeth. Tell them that we are going to take the Toughy Tooth Test (page 49). They choose the answer they think is correct by displaying an answer card. (If teachers have not introduced dental health in class, you may want to do the Toughy Tooth Test after you read the story.)

5. Read *How Many Teeth?* It introduces teeth, tells how many we have at various ages, why they fall out and what they do.

Animals Have Teeth, Too

Materials:

- animal cards (see pages 50–51)

- yarn

- *The Tooth Book* by Theo LeSieg

Prepare in Advance: Make copies of the animal cards. Enlarge them to desired size for children to wear around their necks. Attach them to card stock, color and laminate. Punch two holes at the top of each card. String yarn through the holes to make a necklace.

Activity Directions:

1. Talk about how animals have teeth, too. What do students know about animals and their teeth? Share *The Tooth Book* by Theo LeSieg. This book takes a lighthearted look at what animals do with their teeth.

2. Hand out the animal cards. Have the students line up from left to right in order of how many teeth they think the animal has. The class can help decide where each person should stand. After a set amount of time, about 3 minutes, check the student's line-up and correct as needed.

The number of teeth is:

butterfly—0
anteater—0
chicken—0
beaver—20
elephant—26
rabbit—28
cat—30
human—32
gorilla—32
horse—40
bear—42
dog—42
opossum—50
alligator—80
dolphin—100
tiger shark—10,000+ in a lifetime

Resources

Books:

Meet Your Teeth: A Fun, Creative Dental Care Unit for Kids in Grades 1–4 by Linda Schwartz. Creative Teaching Press, Inc., 1996.

Open Wide: Tooth School Inside by Laurie Keller. Henry Holt & Co., 2000. Solid facts about teeth and their care are sprinkled through an imaginary day at Tooth School with Dr. Flossman and his 32 young teeth students.

What to Expect When You Go to the Dentist by Heidi Murkoff. Harper Festival, 2002. Angus the Answer Dog relieves anxiety by equipping children with the answers to questions they may have about going to the dentist.

Web site:

Healthy Teeth
www.healthyteeth.org/
Learning is fun on this colorful site that includes sections on teeth and gums, prevention, cavities, braces, experiments and activities. There is also a teacher's edition.

Brush, Brush, Brush Your Teeth
(Sung to the tune: "Row, Row, Row Your Boat")

Brush, brush, brush your teeth,

Brush them side-to-side.

Brush them up,

Brush them down,

Or decay will make you frown!

Toughy Tooth Test

Read each statement. Allow students a short amount of time to think, then show one of their cards.

1. Babies are born without teeth.

   Yellow. Yes, they only drink liquids at first.

2. Your teeth have different jobs.

   Yellow. Yes, the front are sharp for biting, the back are flat for chewing.

3. Children have more teeth than adults.

   Green. No, adults have 32 teeth, children have about 20 at age five.

4. Baby teeth fall out because they are too small.

   Green. No, they fall out because a new tooth grows up and pushes it out.

5. You should brush your teeth every time you chew something.

   Green. No, but be sure to brush every morning and every night.

6. With good care, your adult teeth should last the rest of your life.

   Yellow. Yes, you begin to get your adult teeth in first grade. Take good care of them.

Animal Cards

butterfly

anteater

chicken

beaver

elephant

rabbit

cat

human (adult)

Animal Cards

gorilla

horse

bear

dog

opossum

alligator

dolphin

tiger shark

Using Graphic Organizers

Reading Skills: To represent text using story maps or graphic organizers.

Grades: 2–5

Purposes: To learn to organize story elements in written form, comprehend the author's meanings in the stories and identify story elements.

Format: Interactive Lesson

Materials:

- large magnetic board (This activity can be drawn on a chalkboard, but it involves a lot of repetition for multiple classes.)

- muslin or other thin fabric

- markers

- newspaper

- story elements on card stock

- small magnetic strips

Prepare in Advance: See the sample graphic organizers and corresponding stories on pages 55–57. For more examples, refer to the professional book list and Web sites on pages 53–54. Select the skill you want to enhance, then draw the appropriate graphic organizer on fabric. Protect the surface underneath with newspaper as the markers may write through the fabric. Write each element of the story on a piece of card stock and attach a magnetic strip to the back. Set up your magnetic board or clear an area on your magnetic chalkboard. Lay the pieces out face up so you can read them to students.

Note: The organizer can also be drawn on poster board and laminated or drawn on the chalkboard.

In a Hurry?

Because my own classes are only 30 minutes including checkout, I often use picture books with my older readers and apply the same concepts used with longer chapter books. Authors whose picture books are very suitable for older students include: Chris Van Allsburg, Eve Bunting, Daniel Pinkwater and Patricia Polacco. (Her book about a family reunion, *When Lightning Comes in a Jar,* would be excellent for this activity.) Sometimes we read excerpts from books and I rely on Gary Paulsen, Barbara Park, Joan Lowery Nixon and Avi among others.

Activity Directions:

1. Attach the piece of fabric to the magnetic surface with two magnets.

2. Explain to the students the literary concept you plan to graph before you read the story. This helps them listen with a "third ear." Explain it again before doing the assignment.

3. Read the story to the students.

4. Distribute the magnetic story elements to the students. Then ask them which elements fit each section of the organizer. The student who has the appropriate strip places it correctly on the organizer.

Practice Makes Perfect

Materials:

• appropriate graphic organizer

• appropriate word strips

Prepare in Advance: Design or copy an organizer that reinforces the comprehension skill of your lesson. Make the appropriate magnetic word strips. Mark the excerpt or have the picture book ready to read.

Activity Directions:

1. Repeat the organizer activity, but this time give students a blank form to fill in before you do it together.

2. Do the activity as a class and have students check their work. If you feel the concept has been mastered, score the papers and give them to the teacher for recording.

Resources

Books:

The Big Book of Reproducible Graphic Organizers: 50 Great Templates to Help Kids Get More Out of Reading, Writing, Social Studies, and More by Jennifer Jacobson. (Grades K–8) Scholastic, 1999.

50 Graphic Organizers for Reading, Writing & More by Linda Irwin-DeVitis, et al. (Grades 4–8) Scholastic, 1999.

Graphic Organizers and Planning Outlines for Authentic Instruction and Assessment by Imogene Forte and Sandra Schurr. Incentive Publications, Inc., 1999.

Great Graphic Organizers to Use with Any Book! by Michelle O'Brien-Palmer. (Grades 2–6) Scholastic, 1999.

Great Teaching With Graphic Organizers: Lessons and Fun-Shaped Templates That Motivate Kids of all Learning Styles by Patti Drapeau. (Grades 2–4) Scholastic, 1999.

Web sites:

Graphic Organizer Generators
www.teach-nology.com/web_tools/graphic_org/
There are five main categories—some of them let you add information on-line to generate a completed organizer and others help you produce a form that can be printed and filled out. The generators are: Concept Web (5 W's and H), Venn Diagram, Timeline and KWL. The SQ3R Chart is a helpful technique for analyzing longer reading passages.

S.C.O.R.E. (Schools of California Online Resources for Education) Language Arts
www.sdcoe.k12.ca.us/score/actbank/torganiz.htm
This site has 17 types of graphic organizers for your adaptation, including clustering, compare/contrast and chain of events.

TeacherVision.com
www.teachervision.com/lesson-plans/lesson-6293.html?s2
This site contains dozens of graphic organizers for every subject. Click on All Subjects or Language Arts. Some of the ELA organizers include: Five Elements of a Story, Vocabulary and 5 W's and an H.

Story Elements Graphic Organizer

Time

Settings

Characters

Suggested Titles:

Mercedes and the Chocolate Pilot by Margot Theis Raven. Sleeping Bear Press, 2002.

Tales from the House of Bunnicula: It Came from Beneath the Bed! Volume 1 by James Howe. Simon & Schuster, 2002.

Story Outline Graphic Organizer

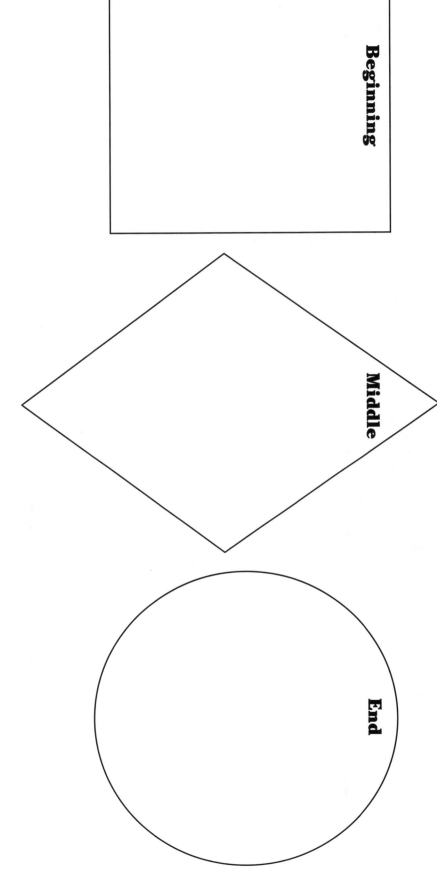

Beginning

Middle

End

Suggested Titles:

First Day, Hooray! by Nancy Poydar. Holiday House, 2000.

The Story of the Titanic by Eric Kentley and Steve Noon. Dorling Kindersley Pub., 2001.

Cause and Effect Graphic Organizer

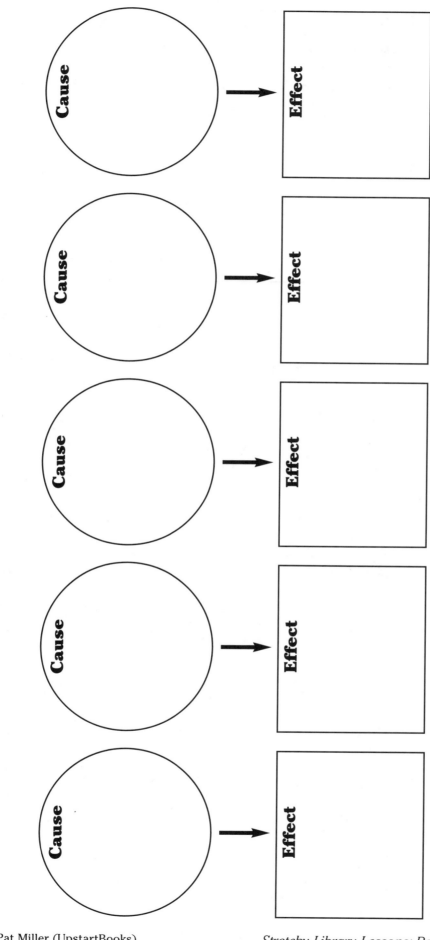

Suggested Titles:

If You Take a Mouse to School by Laura Joffe Numeroff. HarperCollins, 2002.

That's Good! That's Bad! In the Grand Canyon by Margery Cuyler. Henry Holt & Co., 1999.

The Boy Who Cried Wolf

Reading Skills: To draw conclusions, determine cause and effect, retell story in sequence and use setting, characters and story structure to comprehend story.

Grades: K–2

Purpose: To study a fable and its adaptations in order to understand the structure of stories and to write an adaptation of a class or student fable.

Format: Interactive Lesson

Materials:

- *The Wolf Who Cried Boy* by Bob Hartman (Penguin USA, 2002)

- *Betsy Who Cried Wolf!* by Gail Carson Levine (HarperCollins Children's Books, 2002)

- book of Aesop's fables containing "The Boy Who Cried Wolf" or story printed from pbskids.org/lions/wolf/

Prepare in Advance: If you are using this lesson with grade 2, make a transparency of the story "The Boy Who Cried Wolf" so they can read it aloud. For younger students, simply read the story aloud. Prepare a graphic organizer on muslin or chalkboard (see Using Graphic Organizers on page 52). The organizer should include the topics on page 61, written as a blank chart. Display other fairy tale adaptations.

> **Teaching Genres**
>
> Have noted authors teach genres to your students at no charge! Go to Scholastic's Writing With Writers Web site at teacher.scholastic.com/writewit/. Learn to write poetry with Jack Prelutsky, Karla Kuskin and Jean Marzollo. Explore biographies with Patricia and Frederick McKissack or read and write folktales with Nina Jaffe, Alma Flor Ada and Rafe Martin. Jane Yolen will teach your students to write myths, and they can explore fairy tales with Diane Goode.

Activity Directions:

1. Talk about fables and how they explore values. At the "Aesop Fables Online" Web site (www.aesopfables.com/) you will find over 650 fables with morals by Aesop and others.

2. Share the story of "The Boy Who Cried Wolf." Complete the first column on your organizer with student assistance.

3. An adaptation is a version of a tale that intentionally changes at least three important elements. Share *The Wolf Who Cried Boy* with students and have them name at least three things that were changed. What's the same? Complete the second column.

4. As a second lesson, share *Betsy Who Cried Wolf!* Complete the third column, comparing Levine's adaptation to the other two versions.

5. Point out the display of other adaptations. Suggest a folktale or read another fable and ask students how they could change three things.

Fracture Your Own Tale

Grades: 2–5 (You can do the activity with K–1 if you do it as a group and assist with writing.)

Materials:

- a selection from your collection of traditional fairy tales, folktales, fables and Mother Goose rhymes

- worksheet from page 62

Prepare in Advance: Explore the Scholastic site "Writing with Writers: Myths, Folktales & Fairy Tales" at: teacher.scholastic.com/writewit/mff/fairytales_home.htm. You may want to incorporate several of these activities in your lessons. Photocopy the worksheet for your students.

Activity Directions:

1. Have the students work alone, in pairs or in small groups to choose a tale and complete the worksheet. They may want to write their own fractured tale. For ideas have them go to "Writing with Writers: Fractured Fairy Tales and Fables with Jon Scieszka" at: teacher.scholastic.com/writewit/mff/fractured_fairy_about.htm.

2. When students have completed their tales and shared them with the class, allow them time to post their tales on the Scieszka Web site.

Resources

Books:

The Frog Prince—Continued by Jon Scieszka. Penguin Putnam Books for Young Readers, 1994.

Monster Goose by Judy Sierra. Harcourt, 2001. The parodies of 25 favorite Mother Goose rhymes will get your students laughing out loud.

The Stinky Cheese Man and Other Fairly Stupid Tales by Jon Scieszka. Penguin Putnam Books for Young Readers, 2002.

The Three Little Wolves and the Big Bad Pig by Eugenios Trivizas. Simon & Schuster Children's, 1997.

The True Story of the 3 Little Pigs by Jon Scieszka. Penguin Putnam Books for Young Readers, 1996.

Web sites:

The Boy Who Cried Wolf
pbskids.org/lions/wolf/

Writing with Writers: Fractured Fairy Tales and Fables with John Scieszka
teacher.scholastic.com/writewit/mff/fractured_fairy_about.htm

Writing with Writers: Myths, Folktales & Fairy Tales
teacher.scholastic.com/writewit/mff/fairytales_home.htm

The Boy Who Cried Wolf
Graphic Organizer

	The Boy Who Cried Wolf	The Wolf Who Cried Boy	Betsy Who Cried Wolf!
Characters	• boy • townspeople • farmers • wolf • sheep	• Mother Wolf • Father Wolf • Little Wolf • townspeople • farmers • Boy Scouts • sheep	• Betsy • farmers • wolf • sheep
Setting	sheep meadow	wolf's cave	sheep meadow
Problem	The boy tricked the farmers so often that they wouldn't come to help.	The wolf wanted to eat a child instead of his dinner so he yelled "boy." Soon his parents didn't believe him even when a boy sat on the couch.	Betsy cried wolf, but the wolf hid each time so the farmers thought she was trying to trick them.
Solution	The wolf stole all the sheep and the boy learned the value of honesty.	The wolf learned to be honest and to enjoy his mom's home cooking.	The wolf became Betsy's helper and assistant shepherd.
Three things that were changed		1. The boy came to the wolf's house. 2. The wolf cried boy. 3. There were Boy Scouts instead of sheep.	1. The sheep talked in conversation balloons. 2. There was a girl instead of a boy. 3. The wolf became a "good guy."
Author	Aesop	Bob Hartman	Gail Carson Levine

Fractured Fairy Tale Worksheet

Name: _____   Date: _____

Title of the tale you are adapting: _____

You will need to make at least three major changes to the story before you rewrite it. Make your decisions about changes on this sheet

	Original	Your Adaptation
Characters		
Setting		
Time		
Problem		
Solution		

Comprehension Climb

20 MINUTE ACTIVITY

Reading Skills: To respond to questions about story to reflect understanding and use setting, characters, details and main idea to comprehend story.

Grades: K–5, depending on books or series chosen. Questions on pages 65–69 are for the Magic Tree House series, which can be used for grades 2, 3 and less able grade 4 readers.

Purpose: To encourage students to read several books by the same author, to make reading fun in a team situation and to practice comprehension skills.

Format: Team Game

Materials:

- copies of each book featured in the game

- questions (see pages 65–69)

- game board (see example on page 70):

    - foam board (available at craft or hobby stores)

    - silk philodendron plant

    - hot glue or tacky glue

Prepare in Advance: Make the game board by taping the vine of the plant to the center of the board. Every other leaf should be opposite its partner. Use the glue to attach the bottom edge of each leaf to make a pocket. Photocopy the Jack and Annie figures on page 70. Cut them out. Draw a tree house or make one out of cardboard and attach it to the top of the board. Cover the title of each featured book (the covers will be used as a question). Use the questions provided or make up your own. There should be at least four questions per book. If you don't wish to prepare the questions yourself, photocopy page 71 and have the students make up the questions. Award small prizes for each question that is used.

To prepare, you and your teachers can feature the authors, distribute a bibliography and read several of the titles aloud. Buy or borrow multiple copies. If you use Accelerated Reader or Reading Counts, purchase the quizzes for these books as well. Announce the game four to five months in advance so students can read the books. Allow students who have read at least three of the author's listed books to participate.

Activity Directions:

1. The object of the game is to answer the questions correctly in order to help Jack and Annie climb to the Magic Tree House. Divide the class into two teams—Jack and Annie.

2. Take turns asking each team a question. Alternate the book cover questions because they are the easiest. I like to play in a teamwork fashion that includes every child in every question. To reply, a team must discuss the answer among themselves. They agree on an answer and all raise their hands. No one knows which child will be called upon so they must all know the answer. This ensures that no child is left out and no child bears the burden of costing the team a point if an incorrect answer is given.

3. If an answer is incorrect, rebound it to the other team without repeating the question. In this way, both teams are actively listening, everyone is playing and the game is fun even if no prizes are awarded.

4. The teacher or a selected team member is responsible for "climbing" the Jack and Annie figures to the tree house as each question is correctly answered. First team to the top wins.

Onward and Upward

Materials: Same as Comprehension Climb.

Activity Directions:

Play another round, re-starting Jack and Annie at the bottom. When I play this game with my students, 20 minutes is only enough time to get through the first 7 or 8 books. In a subsequent class, we begin another round for the next 7 or 8 books and continue as long as there is interest. Our second grade teachers make Magic Tree House books frequent choices for read-alouds and I tell students about the game early in the school year. The MTH books are so popular that we have three copies of each and students read numerous books in the series in preparation for the game. That is why I extend the game to more than one session.

Resources

Books:

This game works with series books and with assorted books by the same author. You can make up questions for: Dr. Seuss books, Junie B. Jones books, Animorph books, Laura Ingalls Wilder books, Gary Paulsen books, Caldecott books, Henry and Mudge books, etc.

Web site:

Random House Magic Tree House
www.randomhouse.com/kids/magictreehouse/home.html
Includes: Books, Research Guides, Ask the Author, Scrapbook, Readers and Writers Club and Teachers Tree House with book summaries, activities and extension activities.

Magic Tree House Sample Questions

Dinosaurs Before Dark

1. What is the title of this book? (show book jacket with the title covered)
2. How did Jack and Annie (J & A) go back to prehistoric times? (They made a wish on the dinosaur book to see a pteranodon.)
3. What "M" thing did they bring back? (medallion)
4. What did Morgan become so she could help J & A? (Pteranodon)

The Knight at Dawn

1. What is the title of this book?
2. What "M" thing did they bring back? (a blue leather bookmark with an "m")
3. What did Morgan become so she could help J & A? (a knight)
4. How did they get home? (They wished to go home on the Pennsylvania book.)

Mummies in the Morning

1. What is the title of this book?
2. What does Annie find out Egyptian writing is called? (hieroglyphics)
3. What did Morgan become so she could help J & A? (a black cat)
4. What did the ghost queen want? (to be able to go on to the next life)

Pirates Past Noon

1. What is the title of this book?
2. What "M" person did they rescue? (Morgan)
3. What did Morgan become so she could help J & A? (Polly the Parrot)
4. Who is Morgan related to? (King Arthur)

Night of the Ninjas

1. What is the title of this book?
2. What do J & A learn a ninja leader is called? (a ninja master)
3. What thing did they bring back from Japan? (a moonstone)
4. How did they escape from the samurai? (by thinking they were rocks)

Afternoon on the Amazon

1. What is the title of this book?

2. What "M" thing did they have to bring back from the Amazon region? (a red fruit called a mango)

3. What rain forest animal helped them? (a monkey)

4. What did J & A see marching through the rain forest? (army ants)

Sunset of the Sabertooth

1. What is the title of this book?

2. Into whose cave did J & A accidentally stumble? (great bear)

3. What "M" thing did J & A have to find? (a mammoth bone)

4. Who owns the Magic Tree House? (Morgan)

Midnight on the Moon

1. What is the title of this book?

2. What American thing do J & A find on the moon? (an American flag)

3. What was the last "M" thing that J & A had to find? (a mouse)

4. Who is Peanut? (a mouse that is really Morgan under Merlin's spell)

Dolphins at Daybreak

1. What is the title of this book?

2. What does Annie name the two dolphins? (Sukie and Sam)

3. Answer this riddle: Rough and gray as rock, plain as plain can be. Hidden deep inside, there's great beauty inside me. (an oyster)

4. What is a scientist who studies oceans? (an oceanographer)

Ghost Town at Sundown

1. What is the title of this book?

2. Where do J & A hide from the horse thieves? (in barrels)

3. Answer this riddle: Out of the blue, my lonely voice calls out to you. Who am I? Who am I? (an echo)

4. What do you call a town where all the people have moved away? (a ghost town)

Lions at Lunchtime

1. What is the title of this book?

2. Answer this riddle: I'm the color of gold, and sweet as can be. Beware of the danger that's all around me. (honey)

3. If they solve the riddles of Morgan, what will J & A become? (master librarians)

4. What African animal helped them? (a honey guide or bee)

Polar Bears Past Bedtime

1. What is the title of this book?

2. What do J & A learn the word "igloo" means? (house)

3. Answer this riddle: I cover what's real and hide what's true, but sometimes I bring out the courage in you. (a mask)

4. What animal is extremely important to Arctic people? (seals)

Vacation Under the Volcano

1. What is the title of this book?

2. What is the name of the volcano that erupts? (Mount Vesuvius)

3. Slaves or criminals who fought in the amphitheater were called what? (gladiators)

4. What did J & A rescue from the library at what is now Pompeii? (a scroll)

Day of the Dragon King

1. What is the title of this book?

2. What library were J & A looking for in China? (the Imperial Library)

3. What do J & A see people building? (the Great Wall of China)

4. What was considered China's most valuable secret? (how to make silk)

Viking Ships at Sunrise

1. What is the title of this book?

2. What were J & A to show the wisest person they met? (their secret library cards)

3. Why were the Viking ships called serpent ships? (Because there was a serpent or snake carved on the prow.)

4. What do J & A take for safekeeping? (a book)

Hour of the Olympics

1. What is the title of this book?

2. Which goddess does Jack find out is the goddess of victory? (Nike)

3. Who did they show their Master Librarian cards to? (Plato)

4. How did Annie disguise herself to get into the Olympics? (as a soldier)

Tonight on the Titanic

1. What is the title of this book?

2. Name the two children J & A met on the Titanic. (William and Lucy)

3. What was the first gift? (a silver pocket watch)

4. How did they escape the sinking Titanic? (They found the tree house and wished on the Pennsylvania book.)

Buffalo Before Breakfast

1. What is the title of this book?

2. Who is Teddy? (an enchanted dog)

3. What was the second gift? (an eagle feather)

4. Who tricks J & A into thinking he is a wolf? (Black Hawk)

Tigers at Twilight

1. What is the title of this book?

2. The tree house sends J & A to a forest in what country? (India)

3. Why did the tiger need help? (He was caught in a steel trap.)

4. What was the third gift? (a lotus flower)

Dingoes at Dinnertime

1. What is the title of this book?

2. J & A find out that a joey is the young of what animal? (kangaroo)

3. What disaster struck the Australian grassland? (a grassland wildfire)

4. What was the last gift? (a painting of the rainbow serpent)

Civil War on Sunday

1. What is the title of this book?

2. Why is John the drummer boy so important to Jack? (He is Jack's great-great-great grand-father.)

3. What item gave J & A "something to follow"? (a list of remembrances)

4. Clara Barton helped the injured as a nurse. What was her nickname? (Angel of the Battlefield)

Revolutionary War on Wednesday

1. What is the title of this book?

2. What item gave J & A "something to send"? (a letter from the revolutionary war)

3. Who needs J & A's help to cross the Delaware River? (George Washington)

4. Although they were trying hard to help, what did the American army think J & A were acting like? (spies)

Twisters on Tuesday

1. What is the title of this book?

2. Where is the cellar door hidden in the schoolhouse? (under the rug)

3. What item gave J & A "something to learn"? (a poem from a pioneer school house)

4. Why did Jeb start school at an older age? (he had to help on the farm)

Earthquake in the Early Morning

1. What is the title of this book?

2. Where did the earthquake happen? (San Francisco, California)

3. What special writing gave J & A "something to lend"? (a poem on a piece of wood from two boys who were earthquake victims)

4. Why did J & A need four kinds of writing? (to save Camelot)

Christmas in Camelot

1. What is the title of this book?

2. Who has Camelot under his evil spell? (Mordred)

3. What did the spell do to Camelot? (removed music, celebration and laughter)

4. How did J & A help remove the spell? (They brought back the water of memory and imagination.)

Stage Fright on a Summer Night

1. What is the title of this book?

2. What animal did J & A save? (a bear)

3. What is Morgan's job? (Magical Librarian of Camelot)

4. In which of Shakespeare's plays do J & A star? (Midsummer Night's Dream)

Good Morning, Gorillas

1. What is the title of this book?

2. J & A began a second journey to find a special magic. What was it? (sign language)

3. How did their gorilla book advise them to get close to a gorilla? (act like one)

4. What sign language did the gorilla learn? (I love you)

Patterns for Comprehension Climb

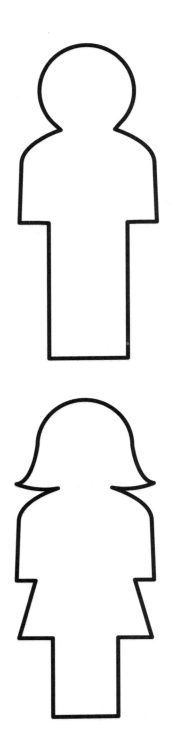

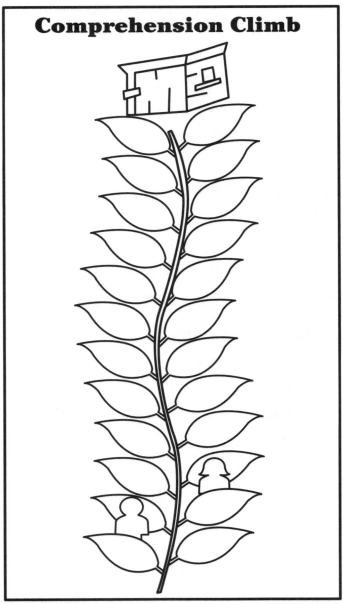

Comprehension Climb

Sample Game Board

Game Piece Patterns: Adjust
size to fit leaves on board.

Student Game Questions

Submitted by: _____   **Teacher:** _____

Questions for the book: _____

You do not need to fill in every question.

1. Why did _____?

   Answer: _____

2. How did _____?

   Answer: _____

3. When did _____?

   Answer: _____

4. What did _____?

   Answer: _____

5. Who _____?

   Answer: _____

6. Where _____?

   Answer: _____

7. Question: _____

   _____?

   Answer: _____

8. Question: _____

   _____?

   Answer: _____

Nonfiction Grabber

Reading Skills: To draw conclusions and make inferences and predictions. To acquire information from books and identify main idea and supporting details.

Grades: K–5, depending on the text used

Purpose: To focus student interest on nonfiction material and to help students listen for facts rather than to hear a story unfold.

Format: Class Participation

Materials:

- question sheet for appropriate book (see pages 75–76)

- *Why Frogs Are Wet* by Judy Hawes for grades K–5

- *The Story of the Titanic* by Eric Kentley and Steve Noon for grades 3–5

Prepare in Advance: Make a photocopy of the questions that correspond with the book you are using. You may write your own questions if you prefer.

Activity Directions:

Why Frogs Are Wet

1. Tell the students they will be using their thumbs to indicate True (thumbs up), False (thumbs down) or I don't know (thumbs parallel to ground). Read the corresponding statements. Have the students show thumbs. When everyone has answered (even if there are some that answer "I don't know"), move to the next question. Do not supply the answer yet.

2. After students respond to all of the questions, read *Why Frogs Are Wet* aloud and answer the questions as you read. This will help the students listen more attentively in order to see if their guesses were correct.

The Story of the Titanic

1. Tell the students they will be using their thumbs to indicate True (thumbs up), False (thumbs down) or I don't know (thumbs parallel to ground). Read the corresponding questions. Have the students show thumbs.

2. When everyone has answered (even if there are some that answer "I don't know"), answer the question with the appropriate part of the book.

3. The questions will whet the students' curiosity and they will want to check out any book on the topic.

Mind Your Q's and A's

Grades: 3–5

Materials:

- questions (see pages 77–78)

- copy of *Why Do Leaves Change Color?* by Betsy Maestro

- chalkboard or chart paper

Prepare in Advance: Make two copies of the question pages. Use one copy for your answer key. Cut the other copy into 24 question cards (do NOT number the cards). Mount each card on card stock or construction paper and laminate for durability. These cards will be handled by each of your classes. Draw a tree on the chalkboard or chart paper.

Activity Directions:

1. This activity can be done after you read *Why Do Leaves Change Color?* to check comprehension or before you read the book to build interest. If the teacher is present, involve him or her in playing the game by keeping score. If there are extra cards, the teacher can have one or two as well. Make sure all of the cards are distributed, even if some players have more than one.

2. The student who has Card 1 reads his or her question (not the answer). He or she should read loudly and distinctly so the entire group can hear.

3. After the student reads his or her card, repeat it if necessary by re-reading it from your answer key. The student who has the corresponding answer card raises his or her hand and responds. If the student is correct, a point is earned for the class. If the answer is incorrect, the point goes to the tree.

4. The student who answered correctly reads the next question and the game proceeds. If a child answered incorrectly, ask "Who has the correct answer, which is … (read from the answer key)." The student who has that answer then reads the next question.

5. You may wish to reward the class if they outsmart the tree with a bookmark, candy or an extra book at checkout time.

Resources

Books:

Fall Leaves Change Color by Kathleen Weidner Zoehfeld. Scholastic Science Readers—Level 1. Scholastic, 2002.

Why Do Leaves Change Color? by Marion B. Jacobs. Rosen Publishing Group, 1998.

Web site:

Spider Tag
www.suzyred.com/2002spidergame.pdf
Print out 26 question and answer cards to accompany Margery Facklam's nonfiction book *Spiders and their Web Sites* (Little, Brown, 2001).

Questions for *Why Frogs Are Wet*

1. Frogs were here on Earth before people. *(True—They have been on Earth for millions of years.)*

2. Frogs can live in water and on land because they are descended from fish that could walk. *(True)*

3. A frog is an amphibian, a Greek word for double life. *(True)*

4. Frogs breathe through their skin and with their lungs. *(True)*

5. There are nearly 900 kinds of frogs. *(False—There are more than 2,000.)*

6. Frogs shed their skin often and eat it. *(True)*

7. Some frogs live their entire lives in water. *(True)*

8. Frogs hibernate in the winter. *(True)*

9. Male frogs sing and female frogs scream. *(True—Frogs were some of the first animals to have a voice.)*

10. Frogs eat insects, dead or alive. *(False—They will starve rather than eat dead bugs. If it doesn't move, they won't eat it.)*

Questions for
The Story of the Titanic

1. How many decks, or levels, were there on the *Titanic*? *(10)*

2. How many months did it take to build the *Titanic*? *(24 plus 10 more to furnish it.)*

3. In what year was the *Titanic's* first, and only, voyage? *(1912)*

4. About how many hundred crewmen were on board to run the ship and serve the passengers? *(900 (899 to be exact)—including French waiters for the Café Parisian—of which 23 were women and 22 were crew who did not sail.)*

5. How many children were on the *Titanic*? *(109)*

6. What flag did the *Titanic* fly? *(A U.S. flag because an American company bought the British White Star line in 1902.)*

7. Did the *Titanic* have elevators? *(Yes, 5)*

8. Were dogs allowed? *(There were so many dogs that a dog show was planned for April 15, the early morning on which the ship sank.)*

9. How many hours did it take for the unsinkable *Titanic* to sink? *(2 hours, 40 minutes—This was the first occasion when the new "SOS" signal was employed.)*

10. How many of the passengers were rescued, by which ship? *(706 passengers were rescued by the* Carpathia, *1,517 died.)*

Question Cards for
Why Do Leaves Change Color?

Card 1

1

A: *You rake them into piles!*

Q: In which season do new leaves sprout on the trees?

A: *Spring*

Q: In which season do the leaves appear to change color?

2

3

A: *Autumn*

Q: What is the job of the green color in leaves?

A: *To soak up the sunlight.*

Q: What is the scientific name for the green coloring?

4

5

A: *Chlorophyll*

Q: How does a leaf take in carbon dioxide from the air?

A: *Through air holes in the leaf.*

Q: Natural colorings like chlorophyll are called what?

6

7

A: *Pigments*

Q: What is the main job of the tree's leaves?

A: *They make a kind of sugar to feed the tree.*

Q: What are three things leaves need to make their food?

8

9

A: *Sunlight, water and air.*

Q: Tree sugar is food to help the tree grow. Where does the tree store extra sugar?

A: *In its leaves.*

Q: What happens in the autumn to tell the trees it's time to get ready for winter?

10

11

A: *There are fewer hours of sunlight each day.*

Q: During what season do the trees rest?

A: *Winter*

Q: As the tree gets ready to rest, the leaves stop making food. Chlorophyll begins to fade. What does that mean?

12

Stretchy Library Lessons: Reading Activities **77**

13

A: *The green color of the leaves begins to disappear.*

Q: Why do leaves appear to change color?

14

A: *When the green disappears, you can see the other hidden colors, or pigments.*

Q: What are three things in nature that have pigment?

15

A: *Bananas, flowers and human skin.*

Q: What makes the leaf have pigments that are red or orange or yellow?

16

A: *Sunlight causes the stored sugar to change to pigment.*

Q: What helps make the leaves have the best fall colors?

17

A: *Sunny days and cool nights.*

Q: What makes the fall leaf colors dull?

18

A: *Too much rain.*

Q: What do you call trees that keep their green leaves all year long?

19

A: *Evergreen trees, like pines and spruce.*

Q: What happens to leaves after they change color?

20

A: *They fall from the tree.*

Q: How do the leaves help the soil?

21

A: *They rot and add minerals to the soil and keep water in the ground.*

Q: What does it mean when trees are dormant in winter?

22

A: *They are resting*

Q: Why are the leaf colors the best in states like New York, Pennsylvania and New Jersey?

23

A: *The temperature and light conditions are just right.*

Q: Do all trees have the same color of fall leaves?

24

A: *No, different trees have different colors.*

Q: What do you have to do after the leaves fall from the trees?

Bibliography

Books:

Auch, Mary Jane. *Peeping Beauty*. Holiday House, 1993.

—. *The Princess and the Pizza*. Holiday House, 2002.

Bate, Lucy. *Little Rabbit's Loose Tooth*. Crown Books for Young Readers, 1983.

Beeler, Selby B. *Throw Your Tooth on the Roof: Tooth Traditions from Around the World*. Houghton Mifflin, 2001.

Bruchac, Joseph. *Between Earth and Sky: Legends of Native American Sacred Places*. Harcourt, 1999.

Clement, Rod. *Grandpa's Teeth*. HarperCollins Children's Books, 1999.

Cohlene, Terri. *Dancing Drum: A Cherokee Legend*. Troll, 1991.

Crummel, Susan Stevens. *Cook-a-Doodle-Doo!* Harcourt, 1999.

Cuyler, Margery. *That's Good! That's Bad! In the Grand Canyon*. Henry Holt & Co., 1999.

dePaola, Tomie. *The Legend of the Bluebonnet: An Old Tale of Texas*. Putnam, 1996.

—. *The Legend of the Indian Paintbrush*. Putnam, 1991.

Dooley, Norah. *Everybody Bakes Bread*. Lerner Publishing Group, 1996.

Drapeau, Patti. *Great Teaching with Graphic Organizers: Lessons and Fun-Shaped Templates That Motivate Kids of all Learning Styles*. Scholastic, 1999.

Facklam, Margery. *Spiders and their Web Sites*. Little, Brown, 2001.

Forte, Imogene and Sandra Schurr. *Graphic Organizers and Planning Outlines for Authentic Instruction and Assessment*. Incentive Publications, Inc., 1999.

Gantos, Jack. *Joey Pigza Swallowed the Key*. HarperCollins Children's Books, 2000.

Gill-Brown, Vanessa. *Rufferella*. Scholastic, 2001.

Hartman, Bob. *The Wolf Who Cried Boy*. Penguin USA, 2002.

Hawes, Judy. *Why Frogs Are Wet*. HarperCollins, 2000.

Hopkins, Jackie Mims. *The Horned Toad Prince*. Peachtree Publishers, 2000.

—. *The Three Armadillies Tuff*. Peachtree Publishers, 2002.

Howe, James. *Tales from the House of Bunnicula: It Came from Beneath the Bed! Volume 1*. Simon & Schuster, 2002.

Irwin-DeVitis, Linda, et al. *50 Graphic Organizers for Reading, Writing & More*. Scholastic, 1999.

Jackson, Ellen. *Cinder Edna*. William Morrow & Co., 1998.

Jacobs, Marian B. *Why Do Leaves Change Color?* Rosen Publishing Group, 1998.

Jacobson, Jennifer. *The Big Book of Reproducible Graphic Organizers: 50 Great Templates to Help Kids Get More Out of Reading, Writing, Social Studies, and More*. Scholastic, 1999.

Johnston, Tony. *The Cowboy and the Black-Eyed Pea*. Putnam, 1996.

Keller, Laurie. *Open Wide: Tooth School Inside*. Henry Holt & Co., 2000.

Kentley, Eric and Steve Noon. *The Story of the Titanic*. DK Publishing, 2001.

Ketteman, Helen. *Bubba, the Cowboy Prince: A Fractured Texas Tale,* Scholastic, 1997

Kleven, Elisa. *Sun Bread*. Penguin Putnam Books for Young Readers, 2001.

LeSieg, Theo. *The Tooth Book*. Random House Books for Young Readers, 2000.

Levine, Gail Carson. *Betsy Who Cried Wolf!* HarperCollins Children's Books, 2002.

Lowell, Susan. *Cindy Ellen: A Wild Western Cinderella*. HarperCollins, 2001.

—. *The Three Little Javelinas*. Northland, 1992.

Maestro, Betsy. *Why Do Leaves Change Color?* HarperCollins, 1994.

Marsh, Valerie. *Beyond Words: Great Stories for Hand and Voice*. Highsmith Press, 1995.

Meddaugh, Susan. *Cinderella's Rat*. Houghton Mifflin, 2002.

Mitchell, Marianne. *Joe Cinders*. Henry Holt & Co., 2002.

Munsch, Robert. *Andrew's Loose Tooth*. Scholastic, 1999.

Murkoff, Heidi. *What to Expect When You Go to the Dentist*. Harper Festival, 2002.

Numeroff, Laura Joffe. *If You Take a Mouse to School.* HarperCollins, 2002.

O'Brien-Palmer, Michelle. *Great Graphic Organizers to Use with Any Book!* Scholastic, 1999.

Osborne, Mary Pope. Magic Tree House series. Random House.

Oughton, Jerrie. *How the Stars Fell Into the Sky: A Navajo Legend.* Houghton Mifflin, 1996.

Perlman, Janet. *Cinderella Penguin.* Penguin Putnam, 1995.

Polacco, Patricia. *When Lightning Comes in a Jar: Come to a Family Reunion.* Putnam, 2002.

Poydar, Nancy. *First Day, Hooray!* Holiday House, 2000.

Raven, Margot Theis. *Mercedes and the Chocolate Pilot.* Sleeping Bear Press, 2002.

Schwartz, Linda. *Meet Your Teeth: A Fun, Creative Dental Care Unit for Kids in Grades 1–4.* Creative Teaching Press, Inc., 1996.

Scieszka, Jon. *The Frog Prince—Continued.* Penguin Putnam Books for Young Readers, 1994.

—. *The Stinky Cheese Man and Other Fairly Stupid Tales.* Penguin Putnam Books for Young Readers, 2002.

—. *The True Story of the 3 Little Pigs.* Penguin Putnam Books for Young Readers, 1996.

Showers, Paul. *How Many Teeth?* HarperCollins Children's Books, 1991.

Sierra, Judy. *Monster Goose.* Harcourt, 2001.

Sturges, Philemon. *Little Red Hen (Makes a Pizza).* Penguin Putnam Books for Young Readers, 2002.

Taylor, C. J. *The Messenger of Spring: A Chippewa, Ojibwa Legend.* Tundra Books, 1997.

Thaler, Mike. *Cinderella Bigfoot.* Scholastic, 1997.

Trivizas, Eugenios. *The Three Little Wolves and the Big Bad Pig.* Simon & Schuster Children's, 1997.

Zoehfeld, Kathleen Weidner. *Fall Leaves Change Color.* Scholastic, 2002.

Web sites:

Aaron Shepard's Reader's Theater
www.aaronshep.com/rt/index.html

Aesop's Fables Online Collection
www.aesopfables.com/

American Sign Language
where.com/scott.net/asl/

Attention Deficit Hyperactivity Disorder
www.brainpop.com/health/nervous/adhd/index.weml

Botham Bakery's Guide to Bread: From Seed to Sandwich
www.botham.co.uk/seed/first.htm

The Boy Who Cried Wolf
pbskids.org/lions/wolf/

Graphic Organizer Generators
www.teach-nology.com/web_tools/graphic_org/

Healthy Teeth
www.healthyteeth.org/

Learn to Sign with Koko
www.koko.org/world/signlanguage.html

Quanah Parker—A Texas Legend
www.lnstar.com/mall/texasinfo/quanah.htm

Random House Magic Tree House
www.randomhouse.com/kids/magictreehouse/home.html

S.C.O.R.E. Language Arts
www.sdcoe.k12.ca.us/score/actbank/torganiz.htm

Spider Tag
www.suzyred.com/2002spidergame.pdf

TeacherVision.com
www.teachervision.com/lesson-plans/lesson-6293.html?s2

TeachingBooks
www.teachingbooks.net

The Texas Comanches
www.texasindians.com/comanche.htm

To Tell the Tooth
www.ada.org/public/games/totell/totelltooth.swf

Writing with Writers
teacher.scholastic.com/writewit/

Writing with Writers: Fractured Fairy Tales And Fables with Jon Scieszka
teacher.scholastic.com/writewit/mff/fractured_fairy_about.htm

Writing with Writers: Myths, Folktales & Fairy Tales
teacher.scholastic.com/writewit/mff/fairytales_home.htm